Anonymous

A Large Collection of Foreign Paintings and Water Colors

Anonymous

A Large Collection of Foreign Paintings and Water Colors

ISBN/EAN: 9783744686457

Hergestellt in Europa, USA, Kanada, Australien, Japan

Cover: Foto ©Thomas Meinert / pixelio.de

Weitere Bücher finden Sie auf **www.hansebooks.com**

No. 247.—Scotch Sheep and Pony in the Mountains. By Eugène Verborckhoven.

CATALOGUE

OF

A LARGE COLLECTION OF

FOREIGN PAINTINGS

AND

WATER COLORS

BELONGING TO

WILLEM F. LAMORINIÈRE

WHO HAS AUTHORIZED AN ABSOLUTE PUBLIC SALE OF THE ENTIRE COLLECTION

ON

Tuesday, Wednesday and Thursday Evenings
December 12th, 13th and 14th

AT EIGHT O'CLOCK

AT THE AMERICAN ART GALLERIES

MADISON SQUARE SOUTH

WHERE THE PAINTINGS WILL BE ON FREE VIEW FROM
THURSDAY, DECEMBER 7TH, UNTIL DATE
OF SALE, INCLUSIVE

THOMAS E. KIRBY
AUCTIONEER

AMERICAN ART ASSOCIATION
MANAGERS

NEW YORK
1899

CONDITIONS OF SALE.

1. The highest Bidder to be the Buyer, and if any dispute arise between two or more Bidders, the Lot so in dispute shall be immediately put up again and re-sold.

2. The Auctioneer reserves the right to reject any bid which is merely a nominal or fractional advance, and, therefore, in his judgment, likely to affect the Sale injuriously.

3. The Purchasers to give their names and addresses, and to pay down a cash deposit, or the whole of the Purchase-money, *if required*, in default of which the Lot or Lots so purchased to be immediately put up again and re-sold.

4. The lots to be taken away at the Buyer's Expense and Risk *upon the conclusion of the Sale*, and the remainder of the Purchase-money to be absolutely paid, or otherwise settled for to the satisfaction of the Auctioneer, on or before delivery; in default of which the undersigned will not hold themselves responsible if the Lots be lost, stolen, damaged, or destroyed, but they will be left at the sole risk of the Purchaser.

5. *While the undersigned will not hold themselves responsible for the correctness of the description, genuineness, or authenticity of, or any fault or defect in, any Lot; and make no Warranty whatever, they will, upon receiving previous to date of Sale trustworthy expert opinion in writing that any Painting or other Work of Art is not what it is represented to be, use every effort on their part to furnish proof to the contrary, failing in which, the object or objects in question will be sold subject to the declaration of the aforesaid expert, he being liable to the Owner or Owners thereof, for damage or injury occasioned thereby.*

6. To prevent inaccuracy in delivery, and inconvenience in the settlement of the Purchases, no Lot can, on any account, be removed during the Sale.

7. Upon failure to comply with the above conditions, the money deposited in part payment shall be forfeited; all Lots uncleared within one day from conclusion of Sale shall be re-sold by public or private sale, without further notice, and the deficiency (if any) attending such re-sale shall be made good by the defaulter at this Sale, together with all charges attending the same. This Condition is without prejudice to the right of the Auctioneer to enforce the contract made at this Sale, without such re-sale, if he thinks fit.

THE AMERICAN ART ASSOCIATION,
MANAGERS.

THOMAS E. KIRBY, *Auctioneer.*

ARTISTS REPRESENTED

Agresti, T., 50.
Anderson, L. W., 87.
Andreotti, F., 153.
Apol, L., 233, 235.
Ardini, G., 17.
Bacca, V. T., 27.
Bail, J., 241.
Ballavoine, J. F., 46, 209.
Barker, W., 93.
Barré, E., 118.
Barzanti, L., 31.
Bauck, A., 89.
Bellei, G., 57.
Berne-Bellecour, E., 135, 211, 232, 262.
Bidau, E., 238.
Binder, A., 121.
Blandford, F., 220, 258.
Blas, V. O., 293.
Bligny, A., 101, 119, 202, 207, 214.
Blincks, T., 245.
Blommers, B. J., 191, 282.
Boddington, H. J., 276.
Bompiani, R., 86.
Bonheur, P., 256.
Boric, J., 105, 117.
Boughton, G. H., 257.
Brandeis, A., 165, 178.
Brument, A., 74.
Buffi, J., 104.
Cacchi, A., 99.
Cameron, E., 5.
Carasii, 288.
Caston, G., 109.

Charpentier, L. F., 145.
Chieostro, C., 61.
Ciachi, Prof. E., 78, 198.
Clays, P. J., 254.
Clisenti, A., 73.
Comini, A., 146.
Corcos, Prof. M. V., 77, 231.
Corradini, A. C., 150.
Costa, Prof. D., 82, 203, 204.
Crochepierre, A., 234.
Crosio, Prof., 149.
De La Mar, D., 94.
De Latour, C., 91, 92.
Delaunay, J., 265.
Delobbe, A., 210, 224, 261.
Demarle, A., 218, 272.
De Mulertt, E., 286.
De Penne, H., 246.
Dillens, P., 24.
Dirckx, A. B., 181, 259.
Eckenfelder, E., 41.
Ehrler, L., 13.
Eiserman, R., 83.
Faby, F., 174.
Farazyn, E., 166.
Fedhmer, E., 53, 130, 142, 184.
Feris, V., 127.
Fraser, R. W., 141.
Friswell, H. P. B., 42.
Gabrini, Prof. R., 64.
Gainsborough, T., 253.
Galiany, E., 12.
Gallon, R., 128.
Gampenreiter, K., 47.

Gassies, G., 11.
Gaucher, E., 26, 156.
Gaucher, C., 182.
Gerard, G., 215.
Gobi, Prof. A., 76, 120.
Groegaert, G., 222.
Groenewegen, A. J., 134, 140.
Grolleron, P., 186.
Gruppe, C. P., 299.
Guena, A., 88.
Guignery, G., 158.
Haeck, L., 98.
Hahn, G., 179.
Halle, C., 159.
Hamilton, G., 2.
Harrison, B., 100.
Hass, F., 14.
Heger, L., 55.
Heilbuth, F., 137, 225.
Hens, F., 16, 51, 116, 129, 144, 172.
Hermans, J. V., 52, 171, 173, 180.
Hernandez, D., 34.
Hews, H., 113.
Hochberger, A., 85.
Holyoake, W., 43.
Hosh, Prof. A., 33.
Hough, W., 124.
Inderiaz, M., 58.
Indoni, Professor, 69.
Innes, G., 194.
Isabey, E., 247.
Jacque, C. E., 187, 212, 274.
Jacquet, J. G., 167, 251.
Jaeckel, A., 29.
Janse, F., 54, 60, 68.
Jarcin, E., 20.
Kahn, M., 79.
Koek-Kock, B. C., 192.
Köhler, I., 71.
Kotschenreiter, Prof. F., 1.
Knopf, A., 25.
Krickeldorf, C., 21.
Lambert, L. E., 213, 279.
Lamorinière, F., 278, 300.

Lawrence, Sir T., 275.
Leroy, J., 75, 107, 136, 208.
Livingston, A. W., 18, 196.
Lolliot, M., 4.
Lorch, O., 62.
Madrazo, R. de, 284.
Malempré, L., 95.
Mareen, E., 114.
Maria, F. D., 111.
Maris, W., 242.
Masziera, F., 80.
Mauve, A., 273.
Max, G., 250.
Mazard, A., 56.
Mazotta, Prof. A., 292.
Mendez, M. G., 175.
Miralles, F., 122, 160, 195.
Monticelli, A., 39.
Moreland, G., 112.
Muller, W., 45.
Munier, E., 260, 266, 290.
Muzzioli, Prof. A., 108.
Nehrmann, K., 177.
Nervoort, J. C., 216.
Neuville, B., 157.
Nicol, J. W., 169.
Normandale, N., 131.
Oehring, H., 123.
Oliver, W., 23.
Overbeeck, G., 285.
Orselli, A., 143, 183.
Otto, G., 70, 162.
Paolotti, D. S., 35.
Patek, L., 163.
Perez, A., 81, 96, 170.
Pio Ricci, 176.
Poelenburg, C. Van, 268.
Portielje, G., 206, 217.
Quitton, E., 132, 133, 139, 226, 227, 229.
Raudnitz, A., 161.
Richet, L., 37, 148, 152.
Richter, E., 155.
Rico, M. D., 283.

Ringeisen, E., 6.
Roguski, J., 230.
Rotig, G. F., 59, 63.
Roy, A., 102, 106.
Roybet, F. V. L., 236.
Rousseau, P., 103, 295.
Ruben, F., 147.
Ruger, H., 15.
Santoro, R., 40.
Schackinger, G., 164.
Scheurer, O., 277.
Schiffi, E., 3, 115.
Schmutzler, Prof. A., 67.
Schödl, M., 264.
Semenowsky, E. E., 49, 221, 223.
Senikosky, L., 9.
Shayer, W., 197, 289.
Sherin, B., 294.
Siberdt, E., 190.
Sighriste, G., 267.
Singoni, Prof. A., 84, 199.
Smith-Hald, F., 200, 237, 281.
Sorbi, R., 243, 291, 298.
Stademann, A., 228.
Stark, J., 240.
Steppe, R., 22, 36, 201, 205.
Stettenberg, F., 72.
Stobbearts, J., 66.
Stoppoloni, A., 110.

Thiollet, A., 7.
Thysen, C. J., 255, 269.
Tinquitz, A., 10.
Truesdell, G. S., 65.
Valentini, V., 28.
Valmon, P., 8.
Van Leemputten, F., 168.
Van Marcke, E., 271.
Van Muyden, E., 185.
Van Os, P. F., 97.
Verboeckhoven, E., 151, 189, 244, 296, 297.
Verhas, F., 193.
Vernier, E., 125.
Veyrassat, J. J., 188.
Vickers, A., 126.
Vinea, Prof. F., 219, 239.
Von Thaunz, B., 90.
Vrolyk, J., 280.
Washington, G., 48.
Weber, M., 30.
Weber, T. A., 270.
Weedon, A. W., 19.
Weiland, 287.
Wendt, P., 38.
Westerbeek, C., 154.
Wilson, R., 44.
Wirkner, A., 138.
Worms, J., 249, 263.

CATALOGUE

FIRST EVENING'S SALE

Tuesday, December 12th

At 8 O'clock

AT THE AMERICAN ART GALLERIES

1

KOTSCHENREITER (Prof. F.)　　　　　　　　Munich

Medals at Berlin, Vienna, and Munich. Professor, Royal Academy, Munich.

The Burgomaster

Signed at the left.　　　　　　Height, 9¼ inches; width, 7¼ inches.

2

HAMILTON (G.)　　　　　　　　United States

A Stroll in the Garden

Signed at the left.　　　　　　Height, 9¼ inches; width, 5 inches.

3
SCHIFFI (A.) — Paris
Pupil of Claude Monet.
Spring
Signed at the right. Height, 10¾ inches; length, 14 inches.

4
LOLLIOT (Mathieu) — Paris
Reading Figaro
Signed at the right. Height, 10¼ inches; width, 8¾ inches.

5
CAMERON (E.) — United States
Iron Tail—Indian Chief
Signed at the left. Height, 6¼ inches; length, 9 inches.

6
RINGEISEN (E.) — Munich
Esmeralda
Signed at the left. Height, 10¼ inches; width, 8¼ inches.

7
THIOLLET (A.) — Munich
View near Boulogne
Signed at the right. Height, 9¼ inches; length, 15¼ inches.

8
VALMON (P.) — Paris
Pupil of Robie.
Flowers
Signed at the right. Height, 15 inches; length, 18 inches.

9

SENIKOSKY (L.) — Munich

Environs of Munich

Signed at the right.   Height, 16¾ inches; width, 13¾ inches.

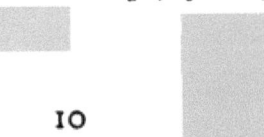

10

TINQUITZ (A.) — Paris

The Bride
(Water color)

Signed at the right.   Height, 17¼ inches; width, 11¼ inches.

11

GASSIES (Georges) — Paris

Landscape near Clichy
(Water color)

Signed at the right.   Height, 11¼ inches; length, 18¾ inches.

12

GALIANY (E.) — Paris

Pupil of Pelouse.   Medals in Limoges and Lyons.

Environs de Bordeaux

Signed at the left.   Height, 18¼ inches; length, 26 inches.

13

EHRLER (L.) — Munich

Still Life

Signed at the left.   Height, 19¼ inches; length, 26 inches.

14

HASS (Fritz) — Munich

Reading the Bible

Signed at the left. Height, 23 inches; width, 16½ inches.

15

RUGER (H.) — Munich

Disconsolate

Signed at the right. Height, 21 inches; width, 16 inches.

16

HENS (Frans) — Antwerp

Peintre de l'Etat Independant du Congo. Pictures in the gallery of the King of Belgium.

Fishermen's Return

Signed at the right. Height, 16 inches; width, 11 inches.

17

ARDINI (G.) — Rome

Monks

Signed at the right. Height, 15 inches; length, 20 inches.

18

LIVINGSTON (Anderson W.) — United States

House of the Last Tribune, Rome

Signed at the right. Height, 24 inches; width, 18 inches.

19

WEEDON (A. W.) — England

Landscape

(Water color)

Signed at the left. Height, 14¼ inches; length, 21 inches.

20

JARCIN (E.) — Paris

"In Clover"

Signed at the left. Height, 21¼ inches; length, 23¼ inches.

21

KRICKELDORF (Carl) — Düsseldorf

La Belle Paysanne

Signed at the left. Height, 29 inches; width, 22 inches.

22

STEPPE (Romain) — Brussels

Medals at Antwerp, Boulogne, and Limoges; pictures in the art galleries of King Leopold of Belgium, Antwerp Museum, and Union League Club, Chicago.

Evening (North Sea)

Signed at the left. Height, 24 inches; length, 32 inches.

23

OLIVER (W.) — England

An Interesting Epistle

Signed at the right. Height, 30½ inches; width, 25 inches.

24
DILLENS (Paul)   Belgium

Environs of Bruges

(From the Antwerp Exhibition of 1898)

Signed at the right.   Height, 21¼ inches; length, 30 inches.

25
KNOPF (A.)   Munich

The New Song

Signed at the right.   Height, 33 inches; width, 22¼ inches.

26
GAUCHER (Ed.)   Paris

Pupil of J. Verwee.

Cattle in Pasture

Signed at the right, 1896.   Height, 23¼ inches; length, 36¼ inches.

27
BACCA VENUTI (Th.)   Rome

Pupil of Osw. Achenbach. Medals at Munich, Leipsic, and Strasburg.

La Femme Aux Cerises

Signed at the right.   Height, 31 inches; width, 19¼ inches.

28
VALENTINI (V.)   Paris

Apple Blossoms

Signed at the right.   Height, 30 inches; width, 23¼ inches.

29
JAECKEL (A.)   Düsseldorf

Monti Pincho, Rome

Signed at the right.   Height, 23½ inches; length, 33 inches.

30
WEBER (M.)   Munich

For Mother's Birthday

Signed at the left.   Height, 29½ inches; width, 24½ inches.

31
BARZANTI (L.)   Paris

In the Garden

Signed at the right.   Height, 28 inches; width, 18 inches.

33
HOSH (A., Prof.)   Düsseldorf

The Widow's Consolation

Signed at the left.   Height, 20 inches; length, 25½ inches.

34
HERNANDEZ (Daniel)   Paris

Medals, Paris, Lisbon, and Rome.

The Gardener's Daughter

Signed at the right.   Height, 26 inches; width, 17½ inches.

35

PAOLOTTI (D. Sylvius) — Venice

Member of Academy in Rome and Florence.

Feeding the Pigeons

(Venice)

Signed at the left. Height, 21½ inches; width, 17 inches.

36

STEPPE (Romain) — Brussels

Medals at Antwerp, Boulogne, and Limoges; pictures in the art galleries of King Leopold of Belgium, Antwerp Museum, and Union League Club, Chicago.

On the Schelde River

Signed at the left. Height, 15½ inches; length, 24 inches.

37

RICHET (Léon) — Paris

Pupil of Diaz. Medal, Exposition Universelle, Salon, 1888.

Pond near Fontainebleau

Signed at the right. Height, 15½ inches; length, 23 inches.

38

WENDT (Philip) — Holland

Calm Sea

(Water color)

Signed at the right. Height, 14½ inches; length, 20½ inches.

MONTICELLI (Adolphe), deceased   Paris
The Garden Party
Signed at the right.   Height, 14¼ inches; length, 22¼ inches.

40
SANTORO (Rubens)   Rome

Medals, 1879, 1880. Chevalier of the Order of the Crown of Italy.
Venice
Signed at the right.   Height, 22 inches; width, 17 inches.

41
ECKENFELDER (E.)   Munich

Medals, Paris, Munich, and Berlin.
Carting Water (Germany)
Signed at the left.   Height, 20¼ inches; width, 16¼ inches.

42
FRISWELL (H. P. Bain)   England

Pupil of Bastien-Lepage.
Midday Rest
Signed at the left.   Height, 17 inches; length, 22 inches.

43
HOLYOAKE (W.)   Paris

Member of the Royal Academy.
A Mahometan
Signed at the left.   Height, 20 inches; width, 16 inches.

44

WILSON (Richard, R. A.) — London

A Classical Landscape and Ruins

(From the collection of Gibson Craig, Esq., of Edinburgh)

Signed at the right. Height, 14 inches; length, 21 inches.

45

MULLER (W.) — London

Born, 1812; died, 1845.

Sunset near Abingdon Park, Thames

Signed at the right. Height, 14 inches; length, 21 inches.

46

BALLAVOINE (Julien Frederic) — Paris

Born in Paris. History and genre painter. Pupil of Pils. Medal, 1880, Paris.

La Dame aux Mésanges

Signed at the right. Height, 18¼ inches; width, 15¼ inches.

47

GAMPENREITER (K.) — Düsseldorf

Pupil of the Academy at Munich, Antwerp, and Brussels.

Hawking

Signed at the right. Height, 15¼ inches; length, 19¼ inches.

48

WASHINGTON (Georges) — Paris

Born in Paris. Pupil of the Academy of Fine Arts, Seville, and the École des Beaux-Arts, Paris. Member of the Legion of Honor.

L'Embuscade

(Water color)

Signed at the right. — Height, 14 inches; length, 17¼ inches.

49

SEMENOWSKY (E. Eisman) — Paris

Pupil of Van Beers. Medals, Antwerp, 1870; Liège, 1871; Medal, Salon, 1880.

The Flower Girl

Signed at the left. — Height, 19½ inches; width, 14½ inches.

50

AGRESTI (T.) — Florence

The Grandmother

Signed at the left. — Height, 12 inches; length, 16 inches.

51

HENS (Frans) — Antwerp

Peintre de l'Etat Independant du Congo. Pictures in the gallery of the King of Belgium.

Marine.

Signed at the right. — Height, 16 inches; width, 11 inches.

HERMANS (J. V.) — Antwerp

Pupil of the Academy of Antwerp. Medals in Ghent and Malines.

The Windmill of Calmpthout

Signed at the left.   Height, 10¼ inches; length, 21 inches.

FEDHMER (E.) — Antwerp

First Prize International Concours for Landscape, 1888. Pupil of Van Luppen.

Autumn View near Antwerp

(Water color)

Signed at the right.   Height, 15 inches; width, 10¼ inches.

JANSE (Felix) — Paris

Pupil of Jean Beraud; membre correspondant Cercle Artistique of Antwerp.

Return of the Flock

Signed at the left.   Height, 13 inches; length, 20 inches.

HEGER (Louise) — Brussels

Pupil of Cazin.

Environs of Waterloo (Belgium)

(From the Antwerp Exhibition, 1898)

Signed at the left.   Height, 16 inches; length, 26 inches.

56

MAZARD (A.) — Paris

Medals in Boulogne and Versailles.

A Beautiful Summer Day

Signed at the left. Height, 18 inches; length, 25½ inches.

57

BELLEI (G.) — Rome

Pupil of the School of Fine Arts, Rome. One of the prominent Spanish painters in Rome. Medals at Biscay and Madrid, 1884.

Love at Seventy

Signed at the right. Height, 18 inches; length, 24½ inches.

58

INDERIAZ (M.) — Seville

Professor at Seville.

Orange Harvest in the South of France

Signed at the right. Height, 20½ inches; length, 26 inches.

59

ROTIG (G. F.) — Paris

Pupil of DePenne. Professor at the Academy of Bordeaux.

Waiting for Master

Signed at the right, 1897. Height, 22 inches; length, 26 inches.

60

JANSE (Felix) — Paris

Pupil of Jean Beraud; membre correspondant Cercle Artistique of Antwerp.

Sortie de l'Opera

Signed at the right. Height, 25½ inches; width, 22 inches.

61

CHIEOSTRO (Carlo) — Rome

Born at Gothenberg, Sweden. Pupil of the Academy of Fine Arts, Stockholm, and of Palmaroli, Paris. Medal, Paris, 1879.

A Late Tea

Signed at the left. Height, 28¼ inches; width, 22¼ inches.

62

LORCH (Otto) — Munich

The Happy Seamstress

Signed at the left. Height, 26¼ inches; width, 21¼ inches.

63

ROTIG (G. F.) — Paris

Pupil of DePenne. Professor at the Academy of Bordeaux.

Chiens de Chasse

Signed at the right. Height, 19¼ inches; length, 25¼ inches.

64

GABRINI (Prof. R.) — Rome

Medals, Madrid, Rome, and Paris.

The First Lesson

Signed at the right. Height, 23 inches; width, 17¼ inches.

65

TRUESDELL (G. S.) — England

Return of the Flock

Signed at the right. Height, 15 inches; length, 28 inches.

66

STOBBÆRTS (Jan) — Brussels

Interior of a Dutch Stable

Signed at the right. Height, 20 inches; length, 28 inches.

67

SCHMUTZLER (Prof. A.) — Munich

Professor of the Academy of Munich.

La Toilette de Bal

Signed at the left. Height, 29½ inches; width, 23½ inches.

68

JANSE (Felix) — Paris

Pupil of Jean Beraud; membre correspondant Cercle Artistique of Antwerp.

Auteuil

Signed at the right. Height, 26 inches; width, 22 inches.

69

INDONI (Prof.) — Rome

Popping the Question
(Water color)

Signed at the right. Height, 30½ inches; width, 21½ inches.

70

OTTO (G.) — Munich

Early Vanity

Signed at the right. Height, 31½ inches; width, 26 inches.

71

KÖHLER (I.)   Munich

Spring

Signed at the right.   Height, 36½ inches; width, 21½ inches.

72

STETTENBERG (Fritz)   Munich

The Idol

Signed at the right.   Height, 32 inches; width, 23½ inches.

73

CLISENTI (A.)   Rome

The New Model

Signed at the right.   Height, 32½ inches; width, 24½ inches.

74

BRUMENT (P.)   Paris

Pupil of Joseph Bail.

The Bottle Washer

Signed at the left.   Height, 32 inches; width, 25½ inches.

75

LeROY (J.)   Brussels

Member of the League of Belgian Artists. Medals at Brussels, and Versailles.

Le Coli Postal

Signed at the right.   Height, 26 inches; length, 32 inches.

76

GOBI (Prof. A.) — Rome

The Belle of Sorrento

Signed at the right. Height, 40¼ inches; width, 26¼ inches.

77

CORCOS (Prof. M. V.) — Paris

Born at Livourne. Pupil of Morelli. Medals at Turin, 1880; Milan, 1881. Chevalier of the Orders of St. Maurice and Lazare.

The Lost Treasure

Signed at the right. Height, 44 inches; width, 28 inches.

78

CIACHI (Prof. E.) — Florence

Returning from the Garden

Signed at the left. Height, 45¼ inches; width, 27 inches.

79

KAHN (Max) — Paris

A Russian Interior

(From the Antwerp Exposition, 1898)

Signed at the left. Height, 39 inches; length, 44¼ inches.

80

MASZIERA (F.) — Paris

The Happy Mother

Signed at the right, 1891. Height, 43¼ inches; width, 37¼ inches.

PEREZ (Alonzo) — Paris

Born at Valence, Spain. Pupil of Academy of Paris, and of the École des Beaux-Arts. Member of the Academy of Rome. Medals, Paris, 1878, 1880, Exposition Universelle.

Place de la Concorde, Paris

(14th of July)

Signed at the left.   Height, 46½ inches; width, 33 inches.

COSTA (Prof. D.) — Rome

Born at Florence. Pupil of Tito Conti. Medals, Florence, Turin, Rome, and Naples. Chevalier of the Order of the Crown of Italy.

La Belle Jardinière

Signed at the left.   Height, 47 inches; width, 28 inches.

EISERMAN (R.) — Munich

Feeding the Pigeons

Signed at the left.   Height, 41½ inches; width, 28 inches.

SINGONI (Prof. A.) — Rome

On the Boulevard

Signed at the right.   Height, 43½ inches; width, 27½ inches.

85
HOCHBERGER (A.)   Munich

Medals, Rome, Lisbon, and Vienna.

Still Life

Signed at the right.   Height, 29¼ inches; length, 39¼ inches.

86
BOMPIANI (R.)   Paris

Born, 1850. Pupil of Gamba, Gastaldi, and Fontanasi. Gold medals, Turin, 1872; Diploma of Honor, Florence, in Competitive Congress, 1878; International Exhibition, 1883.

A Patrician Lady

(Water color)

Signed at the left.   Height, 38½ inches; width, 26 inches.

87
ANDERSON (Livingston W.)   United States

St. Mark's Square, Venice

(Night effect)

Signed at the right.   Height, 36½ inches; width, 25½ inches.

88
GUENA (A.)   Madrid

Carmen

(Water color)

Signed at the right.   Height, 39½ inches; width, 20 inches.

89
BAUCK (A.)   Munich
Poppies
Signed at the left.   Height, 28¼ inches; width, 22¼ inches.

90
VON THAUNZ (B.)   Munich
The Sentinel
Signed at the right.   Height, 22 inches; length, 34 inches.

91
DE LATOUR (Chas.)   Paris
See Saw
Signed at the left, 1872.   Height, 20 inches; length, 36 inches.

92
DE LATOUR (Chas.)   Paris
Feeding the Ducks
Signed at the left, 1872.   Height, 20 inches; length, 36 inches.

93
BARKER (Wright, R. A.)   England
Waiting for Master
Signed at the right.   Height, 24 inches; length, 36 inches.

94
DE LA MAR (David)   Holland
Medals, Amsterdam, Rotterdam, and Brussels.
Returning from the Field
Signed at the left.   Height, 31½ inches; ; width, 20¼ inches.

95
MALEMPRÉ (Leo) — Paris

Pupil of Bouguereau and the École des Beaux-Arts.

A Flower Harvest

Signed at the right. Height, 27¼ inches; width, 20¼ inches.

96
PEREZ (Alonzo) — Paris

Born at Valence, Spain. Pupil of Academy of Paris, and of the École des Beaux-Arts. Member of the Academy of Rome. Medals, Paris, 1878, 1880, Exposition Universelle, 1888.

Une Partie de Campagne

Signed at the left. Height, 22¼ inches; length, 29¼ inches.

97
VAN OS (P. F.) — Holland

Various medals. Teacher of Anton Mauve.

Country Scene

Signed at the left. Height, 22¼ inches; length, 31¼ inches.

98
HAECK (Leopold) — Antwerp

Honorable mention at the Antwerp International Exhibition, 1894.

Potato Gatherers in Flanders
(From the Antwerp Exposition, 1898)

Signed at the right. Height, 34¼ inches; length, 46 inches.

CACCHI (A.)   99   Rome

Professor at the Academy of Rome.

The First Step

Signed at the left.   Height, 24¼ inches; length, 41¼ inches.

100

HARRISON (Birge)   United States

Une Épave

(Exhibited at the Paris Salon)

Signed at the right.   Height, 44 inches; length, 59¼ inches.

SECOND EVENING'S SALE

Wednesday, December 13th

AT 8 O'CLOCK

AT THE AMERICAN ART GALLERIES

101

BLIGNY (A.)   Paris

Pupil of De Neuville. Medals at Versailles and Sydney.

The Old Guardsman

Signed at the right.   Height, $8\frac{1}{4}$ inches; width, $6\frac{1}{4}$ inches.

102

ROY (A.)   Paris

Pupil of Adolph Schreyer.

Return from Work

Signed at the right.   Height, $8\frac{1}{4}$ inches; length, $10\frac{1}{4}$ inches.

103

ROUSSEAU (Philip)   Deceased

Born in Paris, 1812. First exhibited at Salon, 1834. Medals, 1834, 1848, 1855. Legion of Honor, 1852. One of the eight Grand Medals of Honor, Exposition Universelle, Paris, 1867. Died, 1867. Diploma to the memory of deceased artists.

A Feathered Boatman

Signed at the right.   Height, $6\frac{1}{2}$ inches; length, 10 inches.

104
BUFFI (J.) — Munich

A Bavarian Belle

Signed at the right. Height, 9¾ inches; width, 7¼ inches.

105
BORIC (Julien) — Paris

Pupil of Rosa Bonheur.

The Pets

Signed at the left. Height, 10¼ inches; width, 8¼ inches.

106
ROY (A.) — Paris

Pupil of Adolph Schreyer.

The Storm

Signed at the right, 1895. Height, 8¼ inches; length, 10¼ inches.

107
LeRoy (J.) — Brussels

Member of the League of Belgian Artists. Medals at Brussels and Versailles.

A Good Mother

Signed at the right. Height, 9¾ inches; length, 13 inches.

108
MUZZIOLI (Prof. A.) — Rome

President of the Academy of Rome.

Pleasant News

Signed at the right. Height, 10¼ inches; length, 14 inches.

109
CASTON GILBERT (Jules A.) — Paris
A Disagreement
(Water color)

Signed at the left. Height, 12¼ inches; length, 14¼ inches.

110
STOPPOLONI (A.) — Rome
A New Crop
(Water color)

Signed at the left. Height, 7¼ inches; length, 10¼ inches.

111
MARIA (F. D.) — Paris
La Belle du Sud
(Water color)

Signed at the left, 1883. Height, 13 inches; width, 10 inches.

112
MORELAND (George) — England
The Hunter

Height, 9 inches; width, 7¼ inches.

113
HEWS (Harry) — London
Fishing near Mount Lemon
(Water color)

Signed at the left, 1887. Height, 12 inches; length, 18 inches.

114
MAREEN (E.)   Munich

The Little Italian Girl

Signed at the right.   Height, 10 inches; width, 8 inches.

115
SCHIFFI (E.)   Paris

Pupil of Claude Monet.

Winter

Signed at the right.   Height, 10½ inches; length, 14 inches.

116
HENS (Frans)   Antwerp

Peintre de l'État Indepéndant du Congo. Pictures in the gallery of the King of Belgium.

Marine

Signed at the right.   Height, 11 inches; length, 15 inches.

117
BORIC (Julien)   Paris

The Pets' Dinner

Signed at the right.   Height, 8¼ inches; length, 10½ inches.

118
BARRÉ (E.)   Paris

Le Marche aux Fleurs

Signed at the right.   Height, 9 inches; width, 6¼ inches.

119

BLIGNY (A.)   Paris

Pupil of de Neuville. Medals, Versailles, Sydney, etc. Contributor to the Salon.

The Sentinel

Signed at the left.   Height, 8¼ inches; width, 6¼ inches.

120

GOBI (Prof. A.)   Rome

A Good Breakfast

Signed at the right.   Height, 9 inches; length, 12 inches.

121

BINDER (A.)   Munich

Rosalinda

Signed at the left.   Height, 11 inches; width, 9¼ inches.

122

MIRALLES (F.)   Paris

Medals at Paris, Vienna, and Berlin. Medal at International Exhibition, Munich, 1883. Honorable mention, Salon, 1884.

Dolce far niente

(Water color)

Signed at the right.   Height, 10¼ inches; length, 14¼ inches.

123

OEHRING (H.)   Munich

Pupil of Piloty. Medals, Berlin, Vienna, Stuttgart, and Munich.

An Interesting Debate

Signed at the left.   Height, 11 inches; length, 16¼ inches.

124

HOUGH (W.) — London

Pupil of Robie.

Strawberries

(Water color)

Signed at the right.   Height, 10¼ inches; length, 14¼ inches.

125

VERNIER (Émile) — Paris

Landscape

Signed at the right.   Height, 8¼ inches; length, 10¼ inches.

126

VICKERS (Alfred) — London

Born, 1810. English marine and landscape painter. Exhibitor at the Royal Academy and British Institute. Died, 1837.

The Brook

Signed at the right, 1863.   Height, 8¼ inches; length, 12 inches.

127

FERIS (V.) — Madrid

Halt at the Well

Signed at the right.   Height, 9 inches; length, 15 inches.

128

GALLON (R., R. A.) — London

Ross Castle (Sunset)

Signed at the left.   Height, 12 inches; length, 18 inches.

129
HENS (Frans) — Antwerp

Peintre de l'État Independant du Congo. Pictures in the gallery of the King of Belgium.

Storm in the North Sea

Signed at the right. Height, 10½ inches; length, 16½ inches.

130
FEDHMER (E.) — Antwerp

First Prize International Concours for Landscape, 1888. Pupil of Van Luppen.

Winter Scene near Antwerp
(Water color)

Signed at the left. Height, 15 inches; width, 10½ inches.

131
NORMANDALE (N.) — England

Homewards

Signed at the left. Height, 12½ inches; width, 9½ inches.

132
QUITTON (E.) — Antwerp

Pupil of Van Lerius. Member of the Cercle Artistique of Antwerp, and of the League of Belgian Artists.

Still Life

Signed at the right. Height, 14 inches; width, 10½ inches.

133

QUITTON (E.) — Antwerp

Pupil of Van Lerius. Member of the Cercle Artistique of Antwerp, and of the League of Belgian Artists.

Chickens

(Village of Deurne, near Antwerp)

Signed at the right. Height, 13 inches; length, 17½ inches.

134

GROENEWEGEN (A. J.) — Holland

Medals in Amsterdam and Ostende.

Cattle Grazing

(Water color)

Signed at the right. Height, 13 inches; length, 20½ inches.

135

BERNE-BELLECOUR (Étienne) — France

Legion of Honor. Medals, Paris, Lyons, Brussels; represented in the gallery of the Czar of Russia.

For His Country

Signed at the left, 1896. Height, 10½ inches; length, 14½ inches.

136

LeROY (J.) — Brussels

Member of the League of Belgian Artists. Medals at Brussels, Versailles, etc.

Les Amateurs de Confiture

Signed at the right. Height, 12 inches; length, 16 inches.

137

HEILBUTH (F.) — Paris

Officer of the Legion of Honor in 1881; represented in the Luxembourg.

The Trysting Place
(Water color)

Signed at the right.　　　　Height, 17 inches; width, 10 inches.

138

WIRKNER (A.) — Paris

After the Bath

Signed at the left.　　　　Height, 16 inches; width, 10½ inches.

139

QUITTON (E.) — Antwerp

Pupil of Van Lerius. Member of the Cercle Artistique of Antwerp, and of the League of Belgian Artists.

Dead Birds

Signed at the right.　　　　Height, 14 inches; width, 10½ inches.

140

GROENEWEGEN (A. J.) — Holland

Medals in Amsterdam and Ostende.

Cattle in Meadow
(Water color)

Signed at the right.　　　　Height, 13 inches; length, 20½ inches.

141
FRASER (R. W.) — England

Horning Sea-Cambs
(Water color)

Signed at the right, 1898.   Height, 10¼ inches; length, 21¼ inches.

142
FEDHMER (E.) — Antwerp

First Prize International Concours for Landscape, 1888. Pupil of Van Luppen.

Winter Scene

Signed at the left.   Height, 15¼ inches; length, 20¼ inches.

143
ORSELLI (A.) — Rome

Age and Youth
(Water color)

Signed at the right.   Height, 14¾ inches; length, 21¾ inches.

144
HENS (Frans) — Antwerp

Peintre de l'État Independant du Congo. Pictures in the gallery of the King of Belgium.

Marine

Signed at the right.   Height, 11¼ inches; length, 19¾ inches.

145
CHARPENTIER (L. F.) — Paris

In the French Flanders

Signed at the left.   Height, 19¾ inches; length, 24 inches.

146

COMINI (A.) — Munich

Rural Pastime

Signed at the left. Height, 16¾ inches; length, 21 inches.

147

RUBEN (F.) — Paris

Medals at Naples and Vienna.

View in Cairo

Signed at the right. Height, 15 inches; length, 26 inches.

148

RICHET (Léon) — Paris

Pupil of Diaz. Chevalier of the Order of the Crown of Italy. Member of Academy of Fine Arts, Paris. Medal, Exposition Universelle. Medals, Salon, 1880; Rouen, 1883; Nice, 1885.

"La Mare du Diable" (near Fontainebleau)

Signed at the left. Height, 20 inches; length, 26 inches.

149

CROSIO (Professor) — Madrid

First Step

Signed at the left. Height, 16¼ inches; length, 28 inches.

150

CORRADINI (A. C.) — Rome

The Surprise

(Water color)

Signed at the right. Height, 25¾ inches; width, 19 inches.

VERBOECKHOVEN (Eugène) — Belgium

Born at Warneton, Belgium, 1799. Died, 1881. Chevalier and Commander of the Order of Leopold of Belgium. Chevalier of the Order of St. Michael of Bavaria. Chevalier of the Order of Christ of Portugal. Decorated with the Iron Cross. Published in 1822 in the Gallery of the Great Painters of Belgium and Holland. Member of the Academies of Belgium, Antwerp, and St. Petersburg. Medals, 1824, and First Class, 1841. Cross of the Legion of Honor, 1845, Medal, 1885, Exposition Universelle. Hors Concours.

Head of Percheron Horse
(From the Holland Sale of 1898)

Signed at the left, 1856.   Height, 19½ inches; length, 26 inches.

RICHET (Léon) — Paris

Pupil of Diaz. Chevalier of the Order of the Crown of Italy. Member of Academy of Fine Arts, Paris. Medal, Exposition Universelle. Medals, Salon, 1880; Rouen, 1883; Nice, 1885.

Landscape near Rouen

Signed at the right.   Height, 16½ inches; length, 21¼ inches.

ANDREOTTI (F.) — Florence

Pupil of Munich Academy. Several medals.

The Garden Party

Signed at the right.   Height, 24 inches; length, 29 inches.

WESTERBEEK (C.) — The Hague

Homewards

Signed at the right.   Height, 19½ inches; length, 31¼ inches.

155
RICHTER (Èdouard)   Paris

Pupil of E. Hebert and Léon Bonnat. An artist distinguished for his wonderful color schemes. This picture comes from the International Exhibition of Antwerp, 1898.

La Belle du Midi

Signed at the right.   Height, 24½ inches; width, 19½ inches.

156
GAUCHER (Ed.)   Paris

Cattle in Pasture

Signed at the left.   Height, 21½ inches; length, 25½ inches.

157
NEUVILLE (Brunel)   Paris

A Study of Cats

Signed at the left.   Height, 21½ inches; length, 25½ inches.

158
GUIGNERY (Guillaume)   Paris

Environs d'Hastiere

Signed at the right.   Height, 21½ inches; width, 18 inches.

159
HALLE (Charles)   Paris

Pupil of Cazin and the École des Beaux-Arts.

Champ de Coquelicots

Signed at the right.   Height, 18 inches; length, 24 inches.

160
MIRALLES (F.) — Paris

Medals at Paris, Vienna, and Berlin. Medal at International Exhibition, Munich, 1883. Honorable mention, Salon, 1884.

Scene near the Grand Hotel, Paris
(Water color)

Signed at the left. Height, 18¼ inches; length, 21¼ inches.

161
RAUDNITZ (A.) — Munich

Member of the Academy in Munich.

The Bride

Signed at the left, 1891. Height, 29½ inches; width, 16 inches.

162
OTTO (G.) — Munich

Music (Still Life)

Signed at the left. Height, 20½ inches; length, 25 inches.

163
PATEK (L.) — Munich

Professor at the Munich Academy.

Convalescent

Signed at the right. Height, 24¾ inches; width, 19½ inches.

164
SCHACHINGER (Gabriel) — Munich

Medals, Düsseldorf, Paris, and Vienna.

May Blossoms

Signed at the right. Height, 18¾ inches; width, 17 inches.

165

BRANDEIS (A.) Rome

Medals at Venice, Florence, and Rome.

Cathedral Interior

Signed at the right. Height, 16 inches; length, 20 inches.

166

FARAZYN (Edgard) Antwerp

Chevalier of the Order of Leopold of Belgium. Medals, first class, Paris, Barcelona, Adelaide, Sydney, Melbourne, etc.; pictures at the Museums of Antwerp, Melbourne, and Sydney; Professor at the Royal Academy of Antwerp; Member of the Jury, Chicago World's Fair.

On the Coast of Belgium
(Taking in the nets—sun effect)

Signed at the left. Height, 18¼ inches; length, 28¼ inches.

167

JACQUET (Jean Gustave, Fr.) Paris

Pupil of Bouguereau. Medal, 1868; medal, first class, 1875. Chevalier Legion of Honor, 1879. A painter of high repute.

The Belle of the Alps

Signed at the right. Height, 25¼ inches; width, 19¼ inches.

168

VAN LEEMPUTTEN (Frans) Antwerp

Professor of the Royal Academy of Antwerp. Chevalier Order of Leopold and St. Michael of Bavaria. Medals, Paris, Berlin, Antwerp, Brussels, etc.

A Flemish Team

Signed at the right. Height, 18¼ inches; length, 25 inches.

169
NICOL (J. Watson) — London

An Unpleasant Reminder

Signed at the left.   Height, 16 inches; length, 21 inches.

170
PEREZ (Alonzo) — Paris

Born at Valence, Spain. Pupil of the Academy of France, and of the École des Beaux-Arts. Member of the Academy of Rome. Medals, Paris, 1878. Exposition Universelle, 1880.

Showery Morning

Signed at the right.   Height, 22 inches'; width, 11¼ inches.

171
HERMANS (J. V.) — Antwerp

Pupil of the Academy of Antwerp. Medals in Ghent and Malines.

Village of Calmpthout

Signed at the left.   Height, 8 inches; length, 21¼ inches.

172
HENS (Frans) — Antwerp

Peintre de l'État Indépendant du Congo. Pictures in the gallery of the King of Belgium.

Fishing-smacks in the North Sea

Signed at the right.   Height, 11 inches; length, 20 inches.

173
HERMANS (J. V.) Antwerp

Pupil of the Academy of Antwerp. Medals in Ghent and Malines.

In the Polders

(From the Antwerp Exposition of 1898)

Signed at the left. Height, 13 inches; length, 11¼ inches.

174
FABY (F.) Rome

Oriental Life

(Water color)

Signed at the right. Height, 15½ inches; length, 20 inches.

175
MENDEZ (M. G.) Spain

An Æsthetic Swell of the Period

Signed at the right. Height, 19 inches; width, 14 inches.

176
PIO RICCI Florence

Professor of the Academy of Florence.

Desired Moments

Signed at the left. Height, 20¼ inches; width, 14½ inches.

177
NEHRMANN (K.) Munich

A Convivial Party

Signed at the right. Height, 15½ inches; length, 24 inches.

178

BRANDEIS (A.)   Rome

Medals at Venice, Florence, and Rome.

The Baths near Naples

Signed at the right.   Height, 13¼ inches; length, 23 inches.

179

HAHN (Georges)   Munich

Evening Prayer

Signed at the right.   Height, 19¼ inches; width, 14¼ inches.

180

HERMANS (J. V.)   Antwerp

Pupil of the Academy of Antwerp. Medals in Ghent and Malines.

In the Flemish Polders

Signed at the right.   Height, 13 inches; length, 21¼ inches.

181

DIRCKX (Anton B.)   Rotterdam

Medals, Amsterdam, The Hague, Paris, etc.

Canal in Rotterdam

(Water color)

Signed at the left.   Height, 13¼ inches; length, 20¼ inches.

182

GAUCHER (Charles)   Paris

Cattle in Pasture

Signed at the right.   Height, 15¼ inches; length, 18¼ inches.

183

ORSELLI (A.)   Rome

In the Good Old Days

(Water color)

Signed at the right.   Height, 14½ inches; length, 20½ inches.

184

FEDHMER (E.)   Antwerp

First Prize International Concours for Landscape, 1888. Pupil of Van Luppen.

Winter Scene

Signed at the right, 1895.   Height, 14½ inches; length, 19½ inches.

185

VAN MUYDEN (E.)   Paris

A Crouching Tiger

(Water color)

Signed at the right.   Height, 13 inches; length, 18½ inches.

186

GROLLERON (Paul)   Paris

Medals, Paris, 1882, 1886, 1889, 1894. Hors Concours.

En Campagne

Signed at the left.   Height, 16 inches; width, 10 inches.

187

JACQUE (Charles Émile)   Deceased

Born at Paris, 1813. First President of the French Society of Animal Painters. For Designs: Medals, 1851, 1861, and 1863. Cross of the Legion of Honor, 1867. Medal, 1867, Exposition Universelle. For Paintings: Medals, 1861, 1863, and 1864. Cross of the Legion of Honor, 1867. Gold Medal, 1889, Exposition Universelle. Grand Prize, 1889, Exposition Universelle. Hors Concours.

A l'Abreuvoir
(Night effect)

Signed at the left.   Height, 12¼ inches; length, 18¼ inches.

188

VEYRASSAT (Jules Jacques)   Paris

Born at Paris. Medals, 1866, 1869, 1872. Cross of the Legion of Honor, 1877. Hors Concours.

On the Road to the Fair
(Breton horses)

Signed at the left.   Height, 14 inches; length, 19¼ inches.

189

VERBOECKHOVEN (Eugène)   Belgium

Born at Warneton, Belgium, 1799. Died, 1881. Chevalier and Commander of the Order of Leopold of Belgium. Chevalier of the Order of St. Michael of Bavaria. Chevalier of the Order of Christ of Portugal. Decorated with the Iron Cross. Published in 1822 in the Gallery of the Great Painters of Belgium and Holland. Member of the Academies of Belgium, Antwerp, and St. Petersburg. Medals, 1824, and First Class, 1841. Cross of the Legion of Honor, 1845. Medal, 1855, Exposition Universelle. Hors Concours.

Peaceful Life

Signed at the left, 1851.   Height, 14¼ inches; length, 22¼ inches.

190

SIBERDT (Eugène)   Antwerp

Chevalier of the Order of Leopold. Professor of the Academy of Antwerp. Medals in Antwerp, Brussels, Ghent, etc.

Le Repos Inoportun

Signed at the right.   Height, 22½ inches; width, 13 inches.

191

BLOMMERS (B. J.)   Scheveningen

Medal, Exposition Universelle, Paris, 1889.

Preparing Dinner

Signed at the right.   Height, 22 inches; length, 28 inches.

192

KOEK-KOEK (B. C.)   Holland

Chevalier Order of Leopold, 1842; the Legion of Honor and Gold Medal, 1840; Paris, 1842; The Hague, 1843; Order of the Lion of Holland, 1849.

Skating in Holland

Signed B. C. K., 1849.   Height, 23 inches; length, 29 inches.

193

VERHAS (Frans)   Brussels

Gold Medal at the Exposition, Brussels, 1878; Gold Medal at the Exhibition, Paris, 1881; Grand Gold Medal of Honor, Exposition, Vienna, 1882; Gold Medal at the Exposition, Berlin, 1884; Duplicate Grand Medal of Honor, Universal Exhibition, Antwerp, 1885; Grand Gold Medal at the Jubilee Exposition, Berlin, 1886; Chevalier of the Order of Leopold; Chevalier of the Legion of Honor.

The Intruder

Signed at the right.   Height, 30 inches; width, 22½ inches.

INNES (Geo., N. A.), deceased — United States

A Quiet Afternoon

Signed at the right.   Height, 24 inches; length, 36 inches.

MIRALLES (F.) — Paris

Medals at Paris, Vienna, and Berlin. Medal at International Exhibition, Munich, 1883. Honorable mention, Salon, 1884.

Near the Bois de Boulogne

(Water color)

Signed at the right.   Height, 25½ inches; length, 32 inches.

LIVINGSTON (Anderson) — United States

Venice

Signed at the left.   Height, 37 inches; width, 26 inches.

SHAYER (W.) — Deceased

English painter. Was elected a member of the Society of British Artists, 1873. Born, 1788; died, 1879.

The Gypsies' Encampment near the New Forest

(From the Redcliffe Collection)

Signed at the right.   Height, 28 inches; length, 36 inches.

198

CIACHI (Prof. E.) Florence

Various medals.

The Flower Girl

Signed at the right. Height, 41 inches; width, 31 inches.

199

SINGONI (Prof. A.) Rome

Gathering Grapes (Italy)

Signed at the right. Height, 56 inches; width, 35 inches.

200

SMITH-HALD (F.) Norway

Chevalier of the Order of St. Olaf. Chevalier of the Order of Charles III. of Spain. Legion of Honor. Officer de l'Academie. Represented in the Gallerie Nationale du Luxembourg, the Museums of Bordeaux, Rheims, Lille, The Hague, the Metropolitan Museum of Art, New York, the Union League Club, Chicago, etc.

The Return of the Fisherman

(Heyst sur mer, Nord Sea)

From the Antwerp Exposition, 1898, where it held the place of honor.

Signed at the right. Height, 50½ inches; length, 78½ inches.

THIRD AND LAST EVENING'S SALE

Thursday, December 14th

AT 8 O'CLOCK

AT THE AMERICAN ART GALLERIES

201

STEPPE (Romain) — Brussels

Medals, Antwerp, Boulogne, Limoges, etc.; pictures in the art galleries of King Leopold of Belgium, Antwerp Museum, Union League Club, Chicago.

Sunset on the Scheldt

Signed at the left. Height, 6 inches; length, 9 inches.

202

BLIGNY (A.) — Paris

Pupil of De Neuville. Medals, Versailles, Sydney, etc. Contributor to the Salon.

Episode of the French Revolution

Signed at the right. Height, 7¼ inches; length, 9¼ inches.

203

COSTAR (Prof. D.) — Rome

Born at Florence. Pupil of Tito Conti. Medals, Florence, Turin, Rome, and Naples. Chevalier of the Order of the Crown of Italy.

Interior of the Pitti Gallery, Florence

Signed at the right. Height, 7¼ inches; width, 5¼ inches.

204

COSTA (Prof. D.) — Rome

Born at Florence. Pupil of Tito Conti. Medals, Florence, Turin, Rome, and Naples. Chevalier of the Order of the Crown of Italy.

Interior of the Pitti Gallery, Florence
(Companion to the preceding)

Signed at the left.   Height, 7¼ inches; width, 5¼ inches.

205

STEPPE (Romain) — Brussels

Medals, Antwerp, Boulogne, Limoges, etc.; pictures in the art galleries of King Leopold of Belgium, Antwerp Museum, Union League Club, Chicago.

Marine (North Sea)

Signed at the left.   Height, 8¼ inches; width, 10¼ inches.

206

PORTIELJE (Gerard) — Antwerp

Gold medals, London, Brussels, Antwerp, etc. Chevalier of the Order of Leopold, 1883. Member of different Art Societies.

Une Querelle de Jeu

Signed at the right.   Height, 7 inches; length, 9¼ inches.

207

BLIGNY (A.) — Paris

Pupil of De Neuville. Medals, Versailles, Sydney, etc. Contributor to the Salon.

La Bonne Pipe

Signed at the right.   Height, 9¼ inches; width, 7¼ inches.

208

LeROY (J.) — Brussels

Member of the League of Belgian Artists. Medals at Brussels and Versailles.

Cats

Signed at the right.   Height, 8¼ inches; length, 10¼ inches.

209

BALLAVOINE (Julien Frederic) — Paris

Born in Paris. History and genre painter. Pupil of Pils. Medal, 1880, Paris.

La Coquette

Signed at the left.   Height, 9 inches; width, 6¼ inches.

210

DELOBBE (A.) — Paris

Pupil of Bouguereau. Medals, 1874 and 1875. Hors Concours.

The Two Sisters

Signed at the left.   Height, 9¼ inches; width, 7¼ inches.

211

BERNE-BELLECOUR (Etienne) — France

Legion of Honor. Medals, Paris, Lyons, Brussels. Represented in the gallery of the Czar of Russia.

At Rest

Signed at the left.   Height, 6¼ inches; width, 5 inches.

JAQUE (Charles Émile) — Deceased

Born at Paris, 1813. First President of the French Society of Animal Painters. For Designs: Medals, 1851, 1861, and 1863. Cross of the Legion of Honor, 1867. Medal, 1867, Exposition Universelle. For Paintings: Medals, 1861, 1863, and 1864. Cross of the Legion of Honor, 1867. Gold Medal, 1889, Exposition Universelle. Grand Prize, 1889, Exposition Universelle. Hors Concours.

Chickens

Signed at the left. Height, 4¼ inches; length, 6¼ inches.

LAMBERT (Louis Eugene) — Paris

Born in Paris, 1825. Pupils of Delacroix. Medals, 1865, 1866, 1870, 1878. Legion of Honor, 1874.

What is it?

Signed at the right. Height, 6¼ inches; length, 9 inches.

BLIGNY (A.) — Paris

Medals, Versailles, Sydney. Contributor to the Salon.

Aide-de-Camp of the Emperor

Signed at the left. Height, 9 inches; width, 6¼ inches.

GERARD (Gaston) — Paris

La Mascotte
(Water color)

Signed at the right. Height, 10 inches; width, 8 inches.

216

NEERVOORT (Jan C.) — Holland

The Amazon

Signed at the left. Height, 10 inches; width, 7½ inches.

217

PORTIELJE (Gerard) — Antwerp

Gold Medals, London, Brussels, Antwerp, etc. Chevalier of the Order of Leopold, 1883.

"Dis Oui"

Signed at the right. Height, 10½ inches; width, 8½ inches.

218

DEMARLE (A.) — Paris

Arab Horseman
(Water color)

Signed at the left. Height, 11 inches; width, 9 inches.

219

VINEA (Prof. F.) — Florence

Medals, 1859, 1863, and 1864. Cross of the Legion of Honor, 1868. Officer of the Legion of Honor, 1878. Grand Medal of Honor, 1878, Exposition Universelle, Hors Concours. Medal at Vienna Exposition, 1873. Chevalier of the Orders of St. Maurice and St. Lazare, Chevalier and Officer of the Orders of Turkey and Persia, Honorary Professor at the Academies at Parma and Turin.

Signed at the right. Height, 12½ inches; width, 9½ inches.

220

BLANDFORD (Fletcher) — England

Cottage Garden, Stevenson, Berks, England

Height, 12 inches; width, 8 inches.

221

SEMENOWSKY (E. Eisman) — Paris

Pupil of Van Beers. Medals, Antwerp, 1870; Liége, 1871; Medal, Salon, 1880.

Fantaisie

Signed at the right. Height, 12½ inches; width, 9 inches.

222

GROEGAERT (G.) — Paris

Born in Paris. Prize of Rome in Paris. Honorable Mention, 1886. Honorable Mention, Exposition Universelle, 1889.

The Bride

Signed at the left, Paris, 1887. Height, 13 inches; width, 9½ inches.

223

SEMENOWSKY (E. Eisman) — Paris

Pupil of Van Beers. Medals, Antwerp, 1870; Liége, 1871; Medal, Salon, 1880.

A Parisian Belle

Signed at the left. Height, 13 inches; width, 9½ inches.

224

DELOBBE (A.) — Paris

Pupil of Bouguereau. Medals, 1874 and 1875. Hors Concours.

A Talk with Cupid

Signed at the left. Height, 14 inches; width, 10½ inches.

225

HEILBUTH (F.) — Paris

Officer of the Legion of Honor. Represented in the Luxembourg.

Picnic on the Seine

Height, 14¼ inches; width, 10¼ inches.

226

QUITTON (Edouard) — Antwerp

Pupil of Van Lerius. Member of the Cercle Artistique of Antwerp, and of the League of Belgian Artists.

Chickens

Signed at the right. Height, 14 inches; width, 9¼ inches.

227

QUITTON (Edouard) — Antwerp

Pupil of Van Lerius. Member of the Cercle Artistique of Antwerp, and of the League of Belgian Artists.

Still Life

Signed at the right. Height, 15 inches; width, 10¼ inches.

228

STADEMANN (A.) — Munich

Sunset in Winter

Signed at the right. Height, 12¼ inches; length, 18¼ inches.

229
QUITTON (Edouard) — Antwerp

Pupil of Van Lerius. Member of the Cercle Artistique of Antwerp, and of the League of Belgian Artists.

Farmyard

Signed at the left. Height, 12½ inches; length, 17 inches.

230
ROGUSKI (Joseph) — Vienna

Pupil of Kowalzky.

Scene in Hungary

Signed at the left. Height, 15 inches; width, 11¼ inches.

231
CORCOS (Prof. M. V.) — Paris

Born at Livourne. Pupil of Morelli. Medals at Turin, 1880; Milan, 1881. Chevalier of the Orders of St. Maurice and Lazare.

Ready for the Promenade

232
BERNE-BELLECOUR (Étienne) — France

Legion of Honor. Medals, Paris, Lyons, Brussels. Represented in the gallery of the Czar of Russia.

Cavalry versus Cyclism

Signed at the left. Height, 16¼ inches; length, 21¼ inches.

233
APOL (Louis) — The Hague

Evening
(Water color)

Signed at the left. Height, 14¼ inches; length, 21¼ inches.

CROCHEPIERRE (André) — Paris

Pupil of Bouguereau and Robert Fleury. Medal, Paris Salon, 1891.

Fileuse au Repos

(From the International Exhibition of Antwerp, 1898)

Signed at the right, 1895.   Height, 16¼ inches; width, 13 inches.

APOL (Louis) — The Hague

The Old Windmill

(Water color)

Signed at the right.   Height, 14¼ inches; length, 18 inches.

ROYBET (Ferdinand Victor Léon) — Paris

Born at Uzes (Gard), April 20, 1840. Pupil in Lyons, of École des Beaux-Arts. Medal of Salon, 1866.

Mademoiselle de Juani Romani

Signed at the right.   Height, 21¼ inches; width, 11¼ inches.

SMITH-HALD (F.) — Norway

Chevalier of the Order of St. Olaf. Chevalier of the Order of Charles III. of Spain. Legion of Honor. Officer de l'Academie. Represented in the Gallerie Nationale du Luxembourg, the Museums of Bordeaux, Rheims, Lille, The Hague, the Metropolitan Museum of New York, the Union League Club, Chicago, etc.

Sunset in Bergen

(From the Antwerp Exposition, 1898)

Signed at the left.   Height, 16¼ inches; length, 24 inches.

238

BIDAN (E.), deceased · Paris

Born in Vaugirard, 1817. Medals, 1849, 1851. Legion of Honor, 1870. Died, 1888.

Still Life

Signed at the right. · Height, 15 inches; length, 18 inches.

239

VINEA (Prof. F.) · Florence

Medals, 1859, 1863, and 1864. Cross of the Legion of Honor, 1868. Officer of the Legion of Honor, 1878. Grand Medal of Honor, 1878, Exposition Universelle; Hors Concours. Medal at Vienna Exposition, 1873. Chevalier of the Orders of St. Maurice and St. Lazare. Chevalier and Officer of the Orders of Turkey and Persia. Honorary Professor at the Academies at Parma and Turin.

Pensive

Signed at the right, 1892. · Height, 22 inches; width, 16 inches.

240

STARK (James) · London

Stark's Family

(From the collection at Lord Dunnington's Castle)

Height, 19¼ inches; width, 16¼ inches.

241

BAIL (Joseph) · Paris

Member of the Legion of Honor. Represented in the Gallerie Nationale du Luxembourg of Paris.

Trop d'Ouvrage

Signed at the left. · Height, 18¼ inches; width, 15¼ inches.

242

MARIS (Willem)   The Hague

Medals in Amsterdam and Paris.

Milking Time

(Water color)

Signed at the left.   Height, 20½ inches ; width, 14½ inches.

243

SORBI (Raf.)   Florence

Medals, 1859, 1863, and 1864. Cross of the Legion of Honor, 1868. Officer of the Legion of Honor, 1878. Grand Medal of Honor, 1878, Exposition Universelle ; Hors Concours. Medal at Vienna Exposition, 1873. Chevalier of the Orders of St. Maurice and St. Lazare. Chevalier and Officer of the Orders of Turkey and Persia. Honorary Professor at the Academies at Parma and Turin.

The Game of Cards

Signed at the left.   Height, 19½ inches; length, 31 inches.

244

VERBOECKHOVEN (Eugène)   Belgium

Born at Warneton, Belgium, 1799. Died, 1880. Chevalier and Commander of the Order of Leopold of Belgium. Chevalier of the Order of St. Michael of Bavaria. Chevalier of the Order of Christ of Portugal. Decorated with the Iron Cross. Published in 1822 in the Gallery of the Great Painters of Belgium and Holland. Member of the Academies of Belgium, Antwerp, and St. Petersburg. Medals, 1824, and First Class, 1841. Cross of the Legion of Honor, 1845. Medal, 1855, Exposition Universelle. Hors Concours.

Head of an Ewe

Signed at the right.   Height, 16 inches; width, 16 inches.

245

BLINCKS (Thomas) — England

The recognized representative hound and hunt painter of England.

A Difference of Opinion

Signed at the right. Height, 14 inches; length, 18 inches.

246

DE PENNE (H.) — Deceased

Member of the Legion of Honor and the Order of Leopold of Belgium. Medals in Paris, Brussels, and Lyons.

Crossing the River

(Water color)

Signed at the left. Height, 12 inches; length, 18 inches.

247

ISABEY (Eugène) — Deceased

Born at Nancy, in 1767. Pupil of Girardet and Dumont. Painter to Empress Josephine, 1805. Legion of Honor, 1817. Commander, 1853. Also Painter to Charles X.

Baie-de-Palerme

Signed at the right. Height, 15½ inches; width, 12 inches.

248

NORWICH SCHOOL

The Farm House

Height, 11½ inches; length, 19½ inches.

249

WORMS (Jules) — Paris

Born at Paris, 1837. Chevalier of Legion of Honor. Pupil of Lafosse. Made his debut at the Salon of 1859.

A Hasty Departure
(Water color)

Signed at the left. Height, 12¼ inches; length, 16¼ inches.

250

MAX (Gabriel) — Munich

Born in Prague, 1840. Pupil of Engerth at Prague Academy, Blass at Vienna, and Piloty at Munich. Gold medals in Berlin, Munich, etc. Honorary member of Munich Academy and Professor.

Resignation

Signed at the right. Height, 14 inches; width, 10½ inches.

251

JACQUET (Jean Gustave), Fr. — Paris

Pupil of Bouguereau. Medal, 1868; Medal First Class, 1875. Chevalier Legion of Honor, 1879. A painter of high repute.

Sweet as the Rose

Signed at the left. Height, 12¼ inches; width, 10 inches.

252

NORWICH SCHOOL

Church in Cumberland

Height, 13¼ inches; width, 11 inches.

253

GAINSBOROUGH (Thomas), (R. A.), deceased — London

Portrait of Lady Kilmaine

(From the sale of the Hon. Carrington Smith's gallery)

Height, 12 inches; width, 9 inches.

254

CLAYS (Paul Jean) — Brussels

Born at Bruges, Belgium, 1819. Pupil of Gudin, Paris. Medals: Paris 1867 (Exposition Universelle). Legion of Honor, 1875. Medal: 1878 (Exposition Universelle). Officer of the Legion of Honor, 1881.

Boats at Scheveningen

Signed at the right. Height, 12¼ inches; width, 9¼ inches.

255

THYSEN (C. J.) — Holland

Professor of the Academy of Haarlem. Medals, The Hague, Amsterdam, Brussels, etc.

Spinning in Holland

(Water color)

Signed at the left. Height, 14¼ inches; width, 10¼ inches.

256

BONHEUR (Peyrol) — France

Sheep at Fontainebleau

Height, 14¼ inches; width, 10¼ inches.

257
BOUGHTON (G. H.), (R. A.) — England
Faithful

Height, 12½ inches; width, 10 inches.

258
BLANDFORD (Fletcher) — England
Driving Geese
(Wiltshire, England)

Height, 12 inches; width, 8 inches.

259
DIRCKX (Anton B.) — Rotterdam

Medals, Amsterdam, The Hague, Paris, etc.

The Schelde River near Flesingue
(Water color)

Signed at the right. Height, 13 inches; length, 18 inches.

260
MUNIER (Émile) — Paris

Pupil of Lucas and Bouguereau. Honorable mention, 1882. Medals, 1881–1883. Hors Concours.

The Happy Playmates

Signed at the right. Height, 11½ inches; width, 9 inches.

261
DELOBBE (A.) — Paris

Pupil of Bouguereau. Medals, 1874 and 1875. Hors Concours.

The Young Bather

Signed at the right. Height, 12 inches; width, 8 inches.

262

BERNE-BELLECOUR (Etienne) — France

Legion of Honor. Medals, Paris, Lyons, Brussels, etc.; represented in the gallery of the Czar of Russia.

En Conge

Signed at the right.   Height, 13½ inches; width, 10½ inches.

263

WORMS (Jules) — Paris

Born at Paris, 1837. Chevalier of Legion of Honor. Pupil of Lafosse. Made his *début* at the Salon of 1859.

The Lovers

Signed at the left.   Height, 14 inches; width, 10½ inches.

264

SCHÖDL (Max) — Vienna

Professor at the Academy of Vienna.

A Bachelor's Collection

Signed at the left, 1890.   Height, 13½ inches; width, 10 inches.

265

DELAUNAY (J.) — Paris

The Farewell Kiss

Signed at the right.   Height, 13 inches; width, 9 inches.

266

MUNIER (Émile) — Paris

Pupil of Lucas and Bouguereau. Honorable mention, 1882. Medals, 1881-1883. Hors Concours.

Cherry Ripe

Signed at the left. Height, 11¼ inches; width, 8¼ inches.

267

SIGHRISTE (Guido) — Paris

Pupil of Meissonier.

Grenadiers of the First Empire

Signed at the left. Height, 11 inches; width, 8¼ inches.

268

POELENBURG (Cornelius Van) — Holland

Born at Utrecht in 1586. Died 1667. Dutch School. History and genre painter. Pupil of Abraham Bloemaert. Went early to Rome, where he took Elsheimer for his model, and studied Raphael. His small landscapes, enlivened with nymphs or figures, taken from sacred history, are tender in color.

Bathers Watched

(Described in Scribner's "Cyclopædia of Painters and Paintings")

Signed at the left. Height, 9 inches; length, 13¼ inches.

269

THYSEN (C. J.) — Holland

Professor of the Academy of Haarlem. Medals, The Hague, Amsterdam, Brussels.

Happy Mother

(Water color)

Signed at the left. Height, 9¼ inches; length, 12¼ inches.

270

WEBER (Theodore Alexander) — Paris

Medals, Rouen, 1886; Havre, 1886; London, 1871; Philadelphia, 1876.

Fishing Smacks at Dieppe

Signed at the right.   Height, 8 inches; length, 11 inches.

271

VAN MARCKE (E.), deceased — Paris

Pupil of Troyon. Medals, 1867, 1869, 1870, 1878. Legion of Honor, 1872. Medal, Universal Exhibition, 1878. Born, 1827. Died, 1891.

A Normandy Cow

Signed at the left.   Height, 7 inches; length, 8 inches.

272

DEMARLE (A.) — Paris

A French Dragoon
(Water color)

Signed at the left.   Height, 11½ inches; width, 9 inches.

273

MAUVE (Anton), deceased — The Hague

Pupil of Van Oos. Medal, Philadelphia, 1876. Medal, Amsterdam and Vienna. Medal, Paris, 1887. Born, 1838. Died, 1888.

Cow and Ducks

Signed at the left.   Height, 4¾ inches; width, 3¾ inches.

274

JACQUE (Charles Émile), deceased   Paris

Born at Paris, 1813. First President of the French Society of Animal Painters. For Designs: Medals, 1851, 1861, 1863. Cross of the Legion of Honor, 1867. Medal, 1867, Exposition Universelle. For Paintings: Medals, 1861, 1863, and 1864. Cross of the Legion of Honor, 1867. Gold Medal, 1889, Exposition Universelle. Grand Prize, 1889, Exposition Universelle. Hors Concours.

Chickens

Signed at the right.   Height, 3 inches; length, 4¼ inches.

275

LAWRENCE (Sir Thomas, P. R. A.)   Deceased

Born at Bristol, England, 1769. Began to draw crayon portraits at Bath and Oxford, while yet a boy. Settled in London in 1787. Elected a Royal Academician, 1794; became president in 1820. He was knighted by George IV. in 1815, and died in 1830.

Lady Musgrave

(From the collection of Sir Albert Deacon)

Height, 9 inches; width, 7 inches.

276

BODDINGTON (H. J.)   London

The Old Cottage

Height, 8¼ inches; length, 10¼ inches.

277

SCHEURER (Otto) — Munich

Professor of the Academy of Munich. Medals, Berlin, Munich, etc.

Ducks

Signed at the right, 1895. Height, 5¾ inches; length, 14¼ inches.

278

LAMORINIÈRE (François) — Antwerp

Commander Order of Leopold, Belgium. Commander Francis-Joseph, Austria. Officer Legion of Honor. Commander St. Michael of Bavaria. Gold Medals, Antwerp, Brussels, Berlin, Vienna. Diploma of Honor, Exposition Universelle of Paris, 1889.

La Sapinière à Putte

Signed at the right. Height, 9¼ inches; length, 12¼ inches.

279

LAMBERT (Louis Eugène) — Paris

Born in Paris, 1825. Pupil of Delacroix. Medals, 1865, 1866, 1870, 1878. Legion of Honor, 1874.

War at Hand
(Water color)

Signed at the right. Height, 10¼ inches; length, 14¼ inches.

280

VROLYK (Jan) — The Hague

Dutch Cattle and Landscape
(Water color)

Signed at the right. Height, 20 inches; width, 13¼ inches.

SMITH-HALD (F.)   Norway

Chevalier of the Order of St. Olaf. Chevalier of the Order of Charles III. of Spain. Legion of Honor. Officer de l'Academie. Represented in the Gallerie Nationale du Luxembourg, the Museums of Bordeaux, Rheims, Lille, The Hague, the Metropolitan Museum of New York, the Union League Club, Chicago, etc. This picture comes from the Antwerp Exposition, 1898, where it had the place of honor.

Moonlight in Bergen

Signed at the left.   Height, 18¼ inches; length, 29¼ inches.

BLOMMERS (B. J.)   Scheveningen

Medal, Exposition Universelle, Paris, 1889.

Repairing of the Nets

(Water color)

Signed at the right.   Height, 20¼ inches; length, 26¼ inches.

RICO (Martin Diego)   Paris

Pupil of Madrazo. Medal at Paris Exposition, 1878. Chevalier of the Legion of Honor, 1878.

Palazzo Reale, Venice

Signed at the left.   Height, 20¼ inches; length, 29¼ inches.

284

MADRAZO (Raimundo de)   Paris

Born at Rome, July 24, 1841, of Spanish parents. Pupil of his father. Medal, First Class, 1878, Exposition Universelle. Cross of the Legion of Honor, 1878. Gold Medal, 1889, Exposition Universelle. Officer of the Legion of Honor, 1889. Hors Concours. Chevalier of the Order of Christ of Portugal. Chevalier of the Order of the Rose of Brazil. Chevalier of the Order of Charles III. of Spain.

Dolce far niente

Signed at the left.   Height, $27\frac{1}{4}$ inches; width, 22 inches.

285

OVERBEECK (G.), deceased   Brussels

The Interrupted Game

(An exquisitely finished picture)

Signed at the left.   Height, $28\frac{1}{4}$ inches; width, 23 inches.

286

DE MULERTT (Eugène)   Barbizon

Pupil of Jules Breton. Medal, Paris Salon, 1895.

The Harvest

(From the Antwerp Exhibition of 1898)

Signed at the left.   Height, 29 inches; width, 24 inches.

WEILAND   Holland

Medals at The Hague, Amsterdam, and Rotterdam.

The Old Dutch Fireplace

Signed at the right.   Height, 26 inches; length, 30 inches.

288

CARISII known as CAESARIS)   Rome

Portrait of a Lady

(From the collection of Baron Steiger, of Memmingen)

Oval panel, with following inscription: TERESIA COTTIA. CAR. FED. CARISII. VX. 10 Feb. 1653. Nat.

Height, 23¼ inches; width, 20 inches.

289

SHAYER (W.)   Deceased

English artist. Was elected a member of the Society of British Artists, 1873.

The Gypsies

(From the Redleaf Collection)

Signed at the right.   Height, 30 inches; width, 25 inches.

290

MUNIER (Émile)   Paris

Pupil of Lucas and Bouguereau. Honorable mention, 1882. Medals, 1881–1883. Hors Concours.

The Young Seamstress

Signed at the right.   Height, 34 inches; width, 26 inches.

291

SORBI (Raf.)   Florence

Medals, 1859, 1863, and 1864. Cross of the Legion of Honor, 1868. Officer of the Legion of Honor, 1878. Grand Medal of Honor, 1878, Exposition Universelle; Hors Concours. Medal at Vienna Exposition, 1873. Chevalier of the Orders of St. Maurice and St. Lazare. Chevalier and Officer of the Orders of Turkey and Persia. Honorary Professor at the Academies at Parma and Turin.

A Game of Chess

Signed at the right.   Height, 19 inches; length, 31¼ inches.

292

MAZOTTA (Professor A.)   Rome

Professor at the Academy of Rome.

The Young Actor

Signed at the right.   Height, 23¼ inches; length, 31¾ inches.

293

BLAS (V. Olleros)   Naples

Born in Spain. Pupil of Villegas. Medal at Cordova, 1882. Medal at Lyons, 1885. Medal at Rome, 1887.

On the Grand Canal in Venice

(Jour de Fête)

Signed at the right.   Height, 22 inches; length, 36 inches.

294

SHERIN (B.) — England

Pupil of Leader, R. A. Contributor to the Salon and to the Royal Academy.

A Beautiful Afternoon in Kent

Signed at the left. Height, 24 inches; length, 42 inches.

295

ROUSSEAU (Philip) — Deceased

Born in Paris, 1812. First exhibited Salon, 1834. Medals, 1834, 1840, 1855. Legion of Honor, 1852. One of the eight Grand Medals of Honor, Exposition Universelle, Paris, 1867. Died, 1867. Diploma to the memory of deceased artists.

A Good Catch

Signed at the right. Height, 25 inches; length, 39½ inches.

296

VERBOECKHOVEN (Eugène) — Belgium

Born at Warneton, Belgium, 1799. Died, 1881. Chevalier and Commander of the Order of Leopold of Belgium. Chevalier of the Order of St. Michael of Bavaria. Chevalier of the Order of Christ of Portugal. Decorated with the Iron Cross. Published in 1822 in the Gallery of the Great Painters of Belgium and Holland. Member of the Academies of Belgium. Antwerp, and St. Petersburg. Medals, 1824, and First Class, 1841. Cross of the Legion of Honor, 1845. Medal, 1855, Exposition Universelle. Hors Concours.

Scotch Sheep and Pony in the Mountains

Signed at the right, 1858. Height, 29½ inches; length, 43½ inches.

VERBOECKHOVEN (Eugène) — Belgium

Born at Warneton, Belgium, 1799. Died, 1881. Chevalier and Commander of the Order of Leopold of Belgium. Chevalier of the Order of St. Michael of Bavaria. Chevalier of the Order of Christ of Portugal. Decorated with the Iron Cross. Published in 1822 in the Gallery of the Great Painters of Belgium and Holland. Member of the Academies of Belgium, Antwerp, and St. Petersburg. Medals, 1824, and First Class, 1841. Cross of the Legion of Honor, 1845. Medal, 1855, Exposition Universelle. Hors Concours.

Sheep
(Sepia)

Signed at the right, 1872.   Height, 29½ inches; length, 43 inches.

298

SORBI (Raf.) — Florence

Medals, 1859, 1863, and 1864. Cross of the Legion of Honor, 1868. Officer of the Legion of Honor, 1878. Grand Medal of Honor, 1878, Exposition Universelle. Hors Concours. Medal at Vienna Exposition, 1873. Chevalier of the Orders of St. Maurice and St. Lazare. Chevalier and Officer of the Orders of Turkey and Persia. Honorary Professor at the Academies at Parma and Turin.

Pensive

Signed at the right, 1894.   Height, 46 inches; width, 29 inches.

299

GRUPPE (Chas. P.) — The Hague

The Fishermen's Return. Scheveningen

(From the Antwerp Exposition of 1898)

Signed at the right, 1898.   Height, 39 inches; length, 52 inches.

LAMORINIÈRE (François)   Antwerp

Commander Order of Leopold, Belgium. Commander Francis-Joseph, Austria. Officer Legion of Honor. Commander St. Michael of Bavaria. Gold Medals, Antwerp, Brussels, Berlin, Vienna. Diploma of Honor, Exposition Universelle of Paris, 1889.

Dans le bois de Wyneghem, near Antwerp

Signed at the right.   Height, 55¼ inches; width, 40¼ inches.

AMERICAN ART ASSOCIATION,
MANAGERS.

THOMAS E. KIRBY,
Auctioneer.